GHOST HUNTING

Ghost stories and legends from Newark, Nottinghamshire and the East Midlands

ROSEMARY ROBB

© 1992

Illustrations by Dennis Hutton

ISBN 0 946404 47 X

Published by

Wye Valley Press

**Thornbridge Manor, Station Road,
Great Longstone, Near Bakewell, Derbyshire. DE45 1NY
Tel: 01629 640 643**

LOCAL HERITAGE SERIES

. . . . . I sought for ghosts, and sped through many a listening chamber, cave and ruin . . . . .

Percy Bysshe Shelley

CONTENTS

INTRODUCTION

Hunting for ghost stories is a fascinating occupation.

During the past year I have found then in such diverse places as — a deserted battlefield, haunted pub cellars (always welcome venues) an empty hospital ward and a church belfry. (I'm terrified of heights).

Special thanks to Newark born Dennis Hutton for his wonderful illustrations, specially designed and sent from his home in Queensland, Australia — almost by return of post. My thanks also to all the people who have given me help and encouragement.

Stories come from Newark, Nottinghamshire, Lincolnshire and the East Midlands. They were related to me and accepted in good faith. I believe them to be genuine, although some names have been altered by request.

'Ghost Hunting' was written for all the people who asked for more. I hope they will enjoy it.

Chapter I

CHILDREN'S GHOSTS

Ghosts of Gonalston Mill

She came from nowhere! One moment he was driving steadily through the dark fog and the next moment the childish figure was there, right in front of his car. 'It was a little girl dressed in very tattered clothing,' the motorist shivered as he recalled the event. 'She appeared to be cut and bleeding as though from terrible injuries. I slammed the brakes on quickly and jumped out, terrified that I had hit her. Although I searched the area thoroughly, I couldn't believe it, there wasn't a soul in sight.'

Several times the little ghost child has been seen wandering in that spot, near Gonalston Mill in Nottinghamshire, always appearing to be horribly maimed and always disappearing when challenged. Locals believe it could be a child who died through falling into machinery through exhaustion.

During the Industrial Revolution it was common practice to send out orphans and foundlings to work in Industry as cheap labour. In the 18th century this happened to children brought from a workhouse in London to work in the water mill.

The children were housed in the cottages around and soon became a common sight as they traipsed through Gonalston barefooted and mostly in rags. The villagers were not unkind but found it hard enough to feed their own growing families, so the mill children were often undernourished and weak from overwork. Conditions in the mill were appalling and safety measures unknown, so few of them reached maturity.

When a child died through neglect, starvation or overwork, it was hastily buried, without ceremony, in the fields or woods nearby. I was informed that one such field has never been ploughed up, but that generations of farmers have ploughed round the supposed 'burial ground.'

The village Blacksmith said, 'In the 20th century the mill changed over to the process of grinding bones. During the last war a workman on the late shift was found outside early one morning. He was sitting on a gate looking pale-faced and visibly shaking.'

Although the man was reprimanded for leaving his job he said, 'I'll never go back. There's no way you'll get me back inside there. That place is haunted. I've seen the little ghost children with my own eyes.'

After the mill was closed down strange noises were heard. Local people heard the sound of children sobbing, and more ghostly figures were seen after dark.

Attempts made to dismantle the mill only led to frustration. I'm told a contractor who attempted to take on the job of dis-mantling the mill wheel experienced many set-backs; it was almost as if there was a jinx on the place. The mill was only recently modernised.

Nowadays the large red brick building that was once Gonalston Mill looks deceptively peaceful in the daylight. In summertime colourful baskets of flowers swing from the modernised doorway. A handsome ginger cat sprawls leisurely beside the racing mill stream that runs into the Dover Beck.

It would seem that all is well. But the older inhabitants of Gonalston still say if you stand on the bridge over the Dover Beck when the wind blows at night, you can hear the cries of the little children who once perished there.

Ghost at the Vicarage

The running of a vicarage can be very hard work, as Mrs. Creed discovered when she first moved into the vicarage at Coddington, near Newark. But after a few weeks her tasks seem to get lighter, and she began to have the strongest feeling that someone was working beside her.

'Then one day I saw her,' she smiled. 'It was early in the morning and I had just come downstairs when suddenly the figure of a young girl appeared in front of me.'

At first Mrs. Creed, who was half awake and half asleep, did not realise that the child was a ghost — although the room seemed to go cold. 'She had the form of a young servant girl aged about twelve. By the clothes she wore I could tell she came from Victorian times.'

The ghostly child was dressed all in white in a long cotton dress reaching down to her ankles. On top of that she wore a frilled apron with neat tucks running down to the hem.

'She was wearing a white cotton cap or bonnet on her head and her long dark hair was so pretty that I put out my hand to touch it.' Mrs. Creed shivered in rememberence, 'but I could feel nothing — and my hand went right through it.'

The little servant girl must have sensed the lady's feelings because she held out her hands in a gesture of welcome, then she disappeared.

The friendly servant was never **seen** again, but sometimes the family had the strongest feelings that she was still around.

The Boy in the Booking Office

This is the story told to me by Roland Hoggard, to whom I am grateful.

Years ago, before the days of the automatic barrier, the station house at Thurgarton, Nottingham was inhabited by a widow with six children. She was the crossing keeper, and for years she had to rise early to open the gates in order to let the early morning lorries cross over the railway lines.

'One morning I woke up at 4am ready to go on duty,' she told him 'and for some unknown reason I felt depressed and reluctant to move.'

The family's living room seemed to be freezing cold. Although she had lit the fire it didn't seem to make any difference. A movement across the room caught her eye. 'There was shadowy figures coming towards me,' she said. 'I could see a motherly figure holding two little girls by the hand. I could see they were shabbily dressed in Victorian clothes.'

As they moved near she was overwhelmed by a feeling of sadness. 'I knew at once they needed comforting, but when I held my arms out to them they disappeared.' From that moment the room was warm again.

Other strange things were happening in the house. Mike, a relation of the family called unexpectedly and was invited to stay the night — as the house was full his aunt invited him to spend the night on a camp bed in the former booking office Early in the morning Mike woke up to hear a young boy's voice chattering away to him. Thinking it was Liam, his youngest cousin, Mike kept his eyes closed and shouted, 'Get off the bed, I need some sleep.'

The chattering persisted so Mike opened his eyes. He was horrified to find the ghost of a small boy sitting on the end of his bed. 'I knew he was a ghost — when I touched him my hand went right through him" he said.

Mike was so scared that he ran out of the house and refused to go back even to fetch his things. 'I wouldn't go back there for any money,' he shivered.

Another family living in the Station House were startled to hear footsteps in the house, especially on the stairs.

'We started to hear movements in the night,' they said, 'when we knew everyone was tucked up in bed. After a while we realised it always happened at the same time — at about one o'clock in the morning.'

The family took it in turns to keep watch but never actually saw anything. Eventually they got so used to the ghostly footsteps that they simply turned over and went back to sleep.

The Ghost Wore Green Velvet

Where had she come from? Why had he never seen her before?

Years ago a small boy was lying on his bed in a house at Basford Crossings, Nottinghamshire. The boy was slowly recovering from an illness and was feeling very bored with life. So he was pleased, though startled, when he looked up to see a little girl in his bedroom. She was dressed in a long green velvet dress of an earlier period and her dark brown hair hung in ringlets.

The girl did not speak but pointed to the boxed games spread out on his duvet. For a while they played happily then she suddenly disappeared, but re-appeared the next day, and the next.

'When is that little girl coming to play again?' the boy asked when he was eventually allowed to go downstairs.

'Which little girl?' his mother was puzzled.

'You know Mum. The girl who came up to my bedroom.'

'You have been dreaming love,' she said. 'Nobody else as been in the house all week.'

'But she has Mum, she has' he cried. 'I mean the girl in the green velvet dress with the dark ringlets.' He couldn't understand why his mother went suddenly pale and had to sit down.

'Not **that** little girl,' she whispered.

Years later the boy grew up to be a Superintendant of police. 'Why did that little girl's appearance upset you?' he asked his ageing Mum when they were talking about his childhood one day.

'I wouldn't believe our house was haunted,' she told him, 'until you gave me her description. It is said that years ago a girl in a green velvet dress climbed onto a chair to watch children playing in the street. Sadly she fell out of the bedroom window and was tragically killed!'

A Scream in the Night

Several ghosts have been seen at the old Rectory at Cromwell, near Newark. The old house could tell many a tale of its occupants during the last three hundred years.

Who was the little boy that suddenly appeared to a lady visitor as she stood at the foot of the stairs? 'One minute he was there and the next minute he seemed to have vanished without trace', she told Vina Cooke-Chambers the present owner. Both women went back to investigate but the child had seemingly melted away.

In 1984 when Mr. Howard, a guest, was staying at the Rectory he also saw a ghost. He slept in a small bedroom not previously used by the family. (Vina said afterwards that none of her children could get warm in there; even at the height of Summer they said it was freezing cold). In the night Mr. Howard was terrified when he woke to find an old lady bending over his bed. She was moaning and wringing her hands, sobbing 'Oh don't mind the child, he screams a lot.'

Next morning Mr. Howard hurriedly left the house without telling the family what had happened. He said he had been 'Called away.'

Months later the story came out when he was talking to Vina's husband Charles who confessed he had also seen the ghost of an old lady. 'She startled me early one morning,' he said, 'when she materialised in front of me at the top of the stairs. She was dressed in the uniform of a Victorian Nannie.' The lady didn't speak a word. 'She was anxiously looking for someone,' he vowed.

I wonder if she was looking for the little ghost boy. Could he be the child that 'screams a lot?'

The ghost of a distressed servant girl has been spotted on the outside of the Rectory attempting to hurry up the front steps, but the Master will not let her into the house. What is he afraid of? The old house could tell.

Chapter II

GHOSTS OF AIRMEN

The ghosts of airmen are numerous, not surprisingly as so many brave young men had their lives cut short at a very early age in the second world war between 1939-45. So many sad epitaphs record the deaths of airmen who had not even reached their eighteenth or nineteenth birthdays. No wonder their spirits are restless, maybe seeking the fulfilment of the life that was denied them.

The East Midlands had its fair share of aircraft stations during the war. Many are the tales of ghostly airmen who still haunt them.

The Phantom Airman

He has been seen by the side of the road many times walking at a brisk pace as though he hadn't a care in the world. He is usually seen at twilight silhouetted against the darkening sky. He travels on the former Fosse Way, and is often spotted quite near to R.A.F. Newton, Notts.

Motorists who have seen the airman have sometimes slowed down to offer him a lift, only to find that as soon as they approach, the apparition disappears.

Could he be the ghost of an airman who was knocked down on that busy road? Or one that was lost on a mission from Newton Airfield?

The Haunted Hanger

Another haunting, I am told, took place at the R.A.F. station at nearby Syerston.

It was noticed that there was an 'atmosphere' in one of the hangers on the airfield, which was reputed to be haunted. Personnel reported that they could sense a 'presence' there, and at times the temperature dropped suddenly. But the mystery deepened one night when lights were seen to go on and off in a locked hanger, which even guard dogs would not enter.

The Pilot Returns

He has been seen many times walking slowly towards the control tower across the airfield at East Kirkby, Lincolnshire. Onlookers have told how

a ghostly pilot silently drags his parachute behind him, his head bowed in sorrow for his companions who died with him after their B17 aircraft crashed in flames on a nearby hillside.

The control tower at R.A.F. East Kirkby — now the Aviation Heritage Centre — seems to be the scene of many ghostly tales stemming from the last war. Ron, an employee of the Centre, told of the shock he had late one evening when he was coming out of the giant hanger. 'No one else was on the premises,' he said. 'I suddenly became aware that a uniformed airman in a peaked cap was walking slowly towards the control tower, but there was something very strange about his movements. I followed him inside the building. Usually there was a warm atmosphere, but this time I was freezing.' Although he searched the building thoroughly the man had vanished.

The next day Ron reported the incident to be told 'It has happened to others before, and always the airman disappears.'

After the pilot was again seen dragging his parachute a Medium was called to the scene to investigate. She insisted that the ghost was named HARRY. An investigation of East Kirkby's records showed that a pilot with the Christian name of Harry **was** missing from the crashed B17.

Ron told me that he had a very strange experience after the war. He had been ordered to move a bomber back to the base at East Kirkby which was to him, 'all in a day's work.' But halfway back to base he was nearly

11

frightened out of his wits. 'I suddenly got the feeling that there was someone standing behind me, then someone or something tapped me on the shoulder. But there was nobody standing there!

Ron tried to tell himself that it was all in his imagination, but he was not convinced. His hands started to shake when he heard a voice behind him. He knew that the radio was switched off. 'After that there was a buzz of conversation all around me,' he said. 'I just couldn't make out the actual words but I could hear the voices clearly. Then, just as suddenly, all was quiet again.'

For a while Ron was shaken by his experience. 'When I had calmed down I wondered if I had tuned in to the voices of a crew that had been killed in that plane during the war. I shall certainly never forget them.'

The East Kirkby Aviation Centre has been set out to resemble the airfield as it was during the war, complete with planes, air-raid shelter, NAAFI, hangers, the restored aforementioned control tower, and another hanger that houses a giant Lancaster bomber. The latter is of course very rare and closely guarded, it is the job of Frank, another employee, to see that the hanger is locked up for the night.

'In August 1989 I had a bit of a shake-up' he said. 'Night after night I have gone through the usual routine without any problems. At closing time I always have a walk round the **inside** of this hanger to make sure it is clear of visitors, then switch all the lights off from the inside and lock the outside doors. On this particular night everything seemed normal until I had closed and locked all the outside doors — then I was astonished to see a bright golden beam of light shine out from inside the hanger. Nobody could possibly have got inside, and the light came on **immediately** which was strange as the fluorescent system takes several seconds to light up.'

The system was checked and proved not to be faulty. Was yet another ghostly airman at work?

A Message from Fred

'There is nothing sinister about our ghost,' Ann Penfold laughed. Ann is the proprietor of the 'Boundary Cafe' at Coleby Grange, Lincolnshire, and like her assistant firmly believes in 'Fred' as they call the ghostly airman who haunts the cafe. She has seen him many times and is not frightened by him at all. 'He only wants to be friendly,' she smiled.

She described Fred as 'a young man no more than 19 or 20, who has dark brown hair parted down the middle in an R.A.F. haircut. He smiles at me with beautiful brown eyes,' she said.

Ann's assistant only sees Fred from the knees up. 'I once saw him perched on top of the fridge in the kitchen,' she chuckled.

Ann sees him in full. 'He is usually dressed in a flying suit,' she said. 'It is the style that has a low crutch hanging heavily at the back — and he wears flying boots.'

Both ladies have seen Fred in overalls. They firmly believe that he is the ghost of an airman who was killed during the last war just across from the cafe.

The 'Boundary Cafe' is in a building that was once part of the R.A.F. camp. (The former control tower can still be seen in the field behind it). Several alterations have taken place since those days.

Mrs. Penfold laughed. 'Fred doesn't like change,' she said. 'He appeared several times when we demolished an old bunker attached to this building. I have also seen him in a workshop behind the kitchen door, apparently working at a bench. He looked up — then quickly disappeared.'

His favourite haunting place is the kitchen — which was once the camp's Operation Room. He often makes himself known by moving things on the kitchen shelves. Ann says he has a habit of appearing when she is rolling out pastry. He can also be mischievous, and helps himself to tarts when she has taken them from the oven.

'He can be irritating too,' she frowned, 'specially when I've made a batch of Yorkshire puddings only to find he has moved them. And he leaves bits of metal or plastic on the table.'

'When I'm working,' she mused 'I seem to receive thought waves from Fred. I believe he is trying to tell me his real name. It sounds like Peter or Pieta. I think he was Polish.'

(Records show that the airfield **did** have Polish airmen stationed there. For a time R.A.F. Coleby Grange was used for repairing damaged planes from Digby and Cranwell, and was also used as a night fighter station).

In spite of his mischievous ways Fred proved to be a special friend to the Penfold family while they were away on holiday.

After they had been away for a few days Ann grew restless. 'Something isn't right at home,' she told her husband. 'I have a strong feeling that we must go home straight away.'

Her husband wasn't too keen on cutting their holiday short just because Ann had a premonition that all wasn't well at home.'

'We **must** go,' she insisted, and started to pack.

'When we arrived home the feeling was even stronger,' she said. 'We opened the back door and we could both smell a strong "fishy" smell.'

The couple were just in time to prevent the fuse box from starting a fire. She believes she recieved a message from Fred.

Shadow from the Past

Even those people who scoff at the existence of ghosts have to admit that the behaviour of animals can sometimes indicate the presence of the 'unseen' for animals cannot lie.

Many years after World War II, a local man living in Bardney bought a field adjacent to his garden so that his daughter could exercise her pony. The field changed hands at a bargain price and he was delighted at the purchase. Young Susan couldn't wait for daylight when she had planned to take her beloved Rusty for his first ride. 'Set my alarm early,' she instructed 'so that I can have a ride before the school bus comes by.' But she was due for a disappointment.

When the family woke up there was a heavy mist across the fields. Still determined to ride, Susan saddled Rusty and walked him through her garden gate into the new property. As she started to mount him the pony kicked his heels in the air, whinnying with fright, then pulled back against the hedge as far as he could go.

'I soothed him, and talked to him,' she told her dad later, 'but he refused to move. It was as if something had terrified him. I just finished up by dragging him into the garden by his reins.'

'It was probably the mist,' her father smiled. 'Sometimes the trees and bushes assume weird shapes in that light. We'll try him again when its daylight.'

When Susan woke to blazing sunshine she was impatient to try again. Rusty enjoyed his morning feed then stood quietly while Susan saddled him up. 'Good boy.' Her father slowly opened the gate to the field and talked to him in a soft voice. 'Easy now,'

The sun cast no shadows, it was a perfect summer morning as Rusty moved slowly across the field. Susan began to relax and enjoy her ride. 'I will just take him over to the other side,' she called. But as soon as she moved away from the shelter of the hedge Rusty began to tremble violently. No amount of cajoling or soothing could persuade the animal to approach the middle of the field.

'I almost began to feel there was someone in the way,' Susan said later. 'Although I knew the field was empty apart from ourselves.'

For many weeks the incident remained a mystery — until her father was relating it to a captive audience one night in the pub.

'That field be haunted,' an elderly man spoke out between puffs at his pipe. 'Animals can sense these things.'

'I can't believe that.' Susan's dad was sceptical — until he heard the end of the man's tale.

It was a grusome story. Apparently a plane had taken off from Bardney airfield during the war, and it crash landed in that very field. The unfortunate pilot had been flung out on the far side of the field and his mangled body was found hanging from a tree.

Chapter III

CAVALIERS AND ROUNDHEADS

Tales of Cavalier and Roundhead ghosts are plentiful in the East Midlands. So many soldiers from both sides lost their lives there in the troublesome 17th century.

One such ghost was seen by a fisherman who had been trying his luck under the bridge at Hawton, near Newark, Notts. When he found it was too dark to fish he started to mount his cycle stacked up with his basket, when he heard a horse approaching. As he pulled to one side he was amazed to see the figure of a Cavalier on horseback ride by at terrific speed. Thinking he was dreaming the fisherman held his bike lamp aloft. The ghostly soldier was still crossing the bridge, then seemed to melt away.

'Later on I found out that in the Civil War soldiers **did** camp in a field near to the bridge,' the astonished man told his friends. 'And would you believe, there is still a hole in the oak door of Hawton church where a pistol was fired during the fighting.'

The Runaway Cavalier

A lady motorist travelling between Caythorpe and Fulbeck had to brake sharply one night when her headlights picked out the figure of a man with 'long dark hair' just about to climb over a wall by the road side. At first she thought it was a tramp, then realised he was also wearing the Royalist uniform. He disappeared without trace.

Several times afterwards she experienced 'a cold feeling' when passing the same wall, although she didn't see the ghost again.

A medium visited the spot and confirmed, 'there is a strong aura running along the top of the wall.' The lady believes the motorist saw the ghost of a Cavalier who was murdered there after he had escaped from a skirmish near Newark Castle.

Horses in Belgrave Square

A lady was working in her office in Belgrave Square, Nottingham on her own. Above the clatter of the typewriter she seemed to hear the distinctive sound of horses hooves in the distance. When she stopped typing she realised she was indeed hearing the sound of horses approaching and they seemed to be heading in her direction.

'I was a bit surprised,' she said, 'as we don't often have them in this district.'

Curiosity got the better of her. 'I left my desk and walked to the window to look outside. I couldn't believe my eyes. There were horsemen wearing helmets passing by. But the strangest thing — the helmets were round, similar to those worn by the "Roundheads" in the 17th century. As they bobbed up and down I leaned out of the window. It was daylight and I could clearly see their uniforms, the same uniforms once worn by Cromwell's men.'

As she stared in wonder at the sight the soldiers started to fade. In a moment they had disappeared altogether. 'Then I knew I had seen the ghosts of Roundhead soldiers.'

For a time she wondered if it had all been in her imagination. But as she remembered the sun had been glinting on those helmets in broad daylight, she knew she couldn't have been dreaming.

Months afterwards the lady met a local history fanatic and hesitantly told him of her strange experience. To her relief he wasn't a bit surprised.

'Oh yes,' he said. 'Nottingham was a stronghold for the Parliamentarians during the Civil War. Many Roundhead soldiers were stationed in that house!'

Ghost at the Prince Rupert

'Although it was a bright sunny day outside we were all shivering inside the building,' the workmen said. They were busy in 1978 doing alterations to the former 'Prince Rupert' club in Castlegate, Newark, when they were surprised to feel a sudden drop in temperature. 'Then we heard a heavy tread inside the door at the front, like someone walking about in army boots.'

The foreman went to investigate, suspecting that there might have been intruders on the premises. He couldn't believe his eyes. 'It was a man dressed in the uniform of a Cavalier,' he said. 'It gave me a fright. I knew I was looking at a ghost because I could see right through him!'

Before he had recovered from the shock the apparition had disappeared and the building was warm again.

It is well known that ghosts are restless when their habitat is destroyed in any way, so the landlady of the club was not altogether surprised when she heard that yet another ghost had been seen. Her daughter returned to their home from the club one day looking white and frightened. 'I had just gone into the King's Sconce Lounge' (then used as a Pool Room) she said, 'when I had a premonition that I was not on my own. It was unbelieveable, I was just in time to see the top half of a Cavalier disappearing through the wall,'

The 'Prince Rupert Club' was formerly a 17th century inn then known as the 'George and Dragon' (Referred to in my last book concerning a chapter on 'Witchcraft'). The building still had a very deep well on show in the lounge. This was supposed to have a passage underneath that once ran through to Newark Castle.

Did the ghostly Cavalier once visit the inn to taste the local brew? Or was his visit of a more sinister nature?

The Cavalier Returns

It was a dark windy night. Joan Fretwell was all alone in 'Dijon House,' her home for many years in the village of Laxton in Nottinghamshire. But Joan had no fear as she watched her favourite programme on the television, surrounded by the warmth of those stout walls that had stood for at least 300 years, on foundations that she knew were even older. She knew that her dog was lying in the kitchen and all the doors were locked — so she was totally unprepared for her 'visitor.'

'Halfway through the evening I walked out of my lounge towards the kitchen when I felt something brush against my skirt,' she said. 'At the time I thought it was my dog, but as I absent-mindedly bent down to pat her I had the strangest feeling that I was not alone.'

A noise on the stairs made Joan look up. 'I was just in time to spot a figure standing there. He was dressed like a Cavalier in a black plumed hat, a short black cloak and black stockings. The only thing missing was his sword.'

For a moment Joan was shaken — then curiosity overcame her fear and she followed the man upstairs, only to see him melt away. It was only then that her legs began to tremble and she had to sit down 'In a hurry.'

She confessed 'I have never actually **seen** him again, but only recently I had the same feeling that I was being watched!'

By chance Joan was telling her experience to the local W.I. at one of their meetings. She was surprised when fellow member, Elsie Rayner, turned very pale.

'I had the same experience in this very hall,' she said quietly. 'Fifteen years ago I came in here, as Caretaker, to light the fire and prepare for the meeting that night. I was really terrified when I realised a man in black was standing watching me.' Her voice trembled at the memory. 'He also was wearing a large black hat with a plume in it, a black cloak and sort of dark stockings tucked in his boots. I could see his face quite clearly,' she shivered. Although he was fairly handsome his nose was very prominent. I shall never forget his eyes, staring and staring at me.'

'What did you do? Joan whispered.

'At first I asked him what he was doing there — it all seemed a bit unreal at the time — but he didn't answer. Then I remember propping the door wide open with my mop, in case I had to rush out in a hurry. When I turned round he had disappeared.'

Elsie smiled, 'although I was really frightened at the time I had to see the funny side of it next day. I suddenly realised how much he reminded me of that advert — for Sandemann's Port!'

Twilight at Barton Ferry

During the daytime Barton Ferry, near Attenborough in Nottinghamshire, is a most popular spot, especially for the anglers. In the fishing season they can be seen during the daylight hours sitting contentedly all along the river bank. But at twilight they hurriedly pack away their fishing tackle and the place becomes deserted — apart from the ghosts.

Many a tale has been passed on by those who have heard the sound of jingling harness, the clash of steel, and the dull thud of the horses hooves making their way down to the silent river bank after dusk.

There are those who have claimed to have actually seen the horseman.

'They wear the uniform of Oliver Cromwell's men,' one witness told me. 'You never see their faces, but you can clearly make out their round helmets as their horses wade across the ferry towards St. Mary's church on the opposite bank.'

The ghostly Roundheads are said to move slowly as though they are weary after battle. History tells us that Oliver Cromwell's own daughter, who married General Ireton, lived in a house across the river. 'Ireton House' still stands there. Maybe the soldiers sought refuge there after a local skirmish. Maybe there were some who never reached the other side.

So if you go down to Barton Ferry to try your skill with a fishing rod, watch out for the setting sun, and hurry home before you too are caught up with the ghosts from the past.

Chapter IV

NEWARK HAUNTINGS

The Scent of Violets

Ghosts have not actually been seen in the 'Harvest Bakery' cafe at Newark in Nottinghamshire, but have definitely made their presence known to some of the staff.

One of the strangest occurrences has been the unexplained smell, described by some as 'The scent of lilac' and by others as 'a heavy almost sickly smell of violets.' Apparently this scent is around for a few minutes, then 'just seems to disappear.' It has been noticed in several parts of the building.

One girl said she passed it on the stairs and it was as though someone was breathing violet perfume sweets over her. Yet there was no one else about. Another girl noticed it in the office, and yet another source was in the bakery — although a batch of bread had just come out of the oven. One of the bakers said he had no real sense of smell but he also noticed a 'sickly heavy perfume.'

The room upstairs in the 'Harvest Bakery' that is known as the Prep Room (where the food is prepared) has also been the scene of strange happenings. Debbie said she had been working there when food was around and the 'strong smell of lilac had drifted in and overpowered all other smells.' (No polish or aerosol had been used there, and nobody in the room had been using scent). Another girl called Ethel was working alone in the same room when she was startled by a 'black shadowy thing' that passed by her then vanished.

A baker also had a strange experience early one morning when he was hard at work. He said he was alone in the building when he was startled to hear footsteps overhead. 'It was almost as though someone or something was running above the ceiling.'

He plucked up his courage and went upstairs to investigate the attics, but they were completely empty.

A girl had occasion to fetch something from the office upstairs when the door was propped open with a heavy weight. As she passed through she said 'the door suddenly started to come at me as though it was being flung in my face by somebody invisible. It frightened me. There was nobody there. It was really uncanny.'

The Harvest Bakery is part of a 16th century house, a most important building, that once housed the Governor of Newark. The Governor's House has witnessed much of Newark's history through the centuries, including the famous quarrel during the Civil War between King Charles I

19

and his nephew Prince Rupert. From this house the King watched Prince Rupert ride away from Newark Market Place taking his soldiers with him.

Could it be that the building is still haunted by the restless spirit of the King himself? Would the 'heavy, sickly smell' emerge from a pomander carried by a ghostly courtier?

Rumour has it that the skeleton of a man, believed to have been a Royalist soldier, was found years ago in a small upstairs room — now sealed. (I can find no evidence of this, but the story persists).

Who can tell what mysteries surround the old house. Are they all linked by the scent of violets?

The Woman in Black

For months Norah Lunn worked in a Nursing Home on the outskirts of Newark, going about her daily tasks without incident. Then one morning she got quite a shock. She was working in a room which was beside the back door of the Home. The door stood open to let in the warm May sunshine and gave a clear view of the garden.

'One moment there was nobody about,' she said, 'and the next moment there was a strange woman standing in the doorway. I couldn't tell her age as her face wasn't clearly visible — but I could see the long dress she was wearing was black and very dated.'

Visitors to the Home are not allowed inside without permission so Norah waited politely for the woman to state her business — but she did not say a word. Norah gasped when the woman seemed to glide past her, then vanish.

Nobody would believe that Norah had seen a ghost. But a few weeks later when she was beginning to wonder if she had dreamt it, the ghost appeared again. This time several assistants were sorting out patients ironing in the dining room opposite the front door which was open ready for visitors..

'There she is again.' This time Norah called out to the woman in black who was rapidly walking upstairs. Norah was only a few steps behind her and could clearly see the black dress, but to her amazement the apparition vanished on the top step. 'Did you see her this time?' Norah raced back into the dining room. She felt so embarrassed when the staff confessed they hadn't.

She was relieved when the cleaner eventually confirmed that 'a lady in black' had frightened the life out of her, appearing 'from nowhere' when she was cleaning the stairs. Her screams must have frightened the ghostly visitor for she has never been seen again.

Ghosts at the Oliver Cromwell

Kathleen Danks woke up to hear her daughter screaming. 'Mummy,

Mummy, there's a man in my room.'

Kath rushed into her four year old's bedroom with her heart thumping only to find the room was empty, apart from themselves. But the child's cheek's were pallid and she was terrified. 'You've had a bad dream love,' Kath tried to soothe her.

'I haven't Mum, he was **here**' the girl sobbed. 'He was dressed in a black cloak and a funny tall hat. He looked at me with staring eyes — then he disappeared.'

This incident was the first of many unexplained happenings that took place when the Danks family moved into a downstairs flat in an old building in Barnbygate, Newark twenty years ago.

'From the beginning the place had a strange feeling about it,' Kath said. 'We grumbled at our baby-sitter because time after time when we came home from an evening out the back door was unlocked. Yet he was sure he had closed it properly. It couldn't have opened by itself because we had to turn the knob and lift an old-fashioned latch to open it.'

One night she came back to find him trembling in the hallway beside his girl friend. 'There was somebody sitting beside us in the living room," he gasped.

His pale-faced girl friend agreed. 'We couldn't see anyone but we knew somebody, or **something** was there.' Her eyes grew wide. 'Even the dog sensed it and started to quiver.'

They refused to babysit any more, saying 'the house is haunted.'

On a cold winter's night Kath went to call the dog into the warmth of the living room. 'He refused to go in,' she said. 'His hair really did stand on end, and he started to growl — just as if somebody strange was in there.

Next day her friend's dog reacted in the same way and stood whining in the doorway. No amount of coaxing could persuade him to go inside. With a yalp of fear he bolted into the kitchen.

Footsteps were heard on the tiled floor of the kitchen. Nobody was in sight. Once again the door opened by itself, and when Kath went to close to it she felt sure somebody was standing behind her.

The Danks family decided to investigate the history of the house. They were surprised to find that the building stood on the foundations of an ancient inn called 'The Oliver Cromwell Tavern.' Stories had been handed down that a murder had taken place there, it was believved that a soldier had been killed in a drunken brawl.

Kath and her husband decided that they had had enough. They looked desparately for a house of their own. Then one night they had a truly terrifying experience.

'We were sleeping peacefully in our front bedroom overlooking the street,' Kath said. 'Usually we could see the street lamp shining through our curtains but on this occasion we woke to find the room was in darkness. There seemed to be such a atmosphere. We both felt as if we were being stifled, yet we were afraid to move.'

When her husband at last plucked up the courage to try and find the light switch he had the erriest feeling that he was being held back by a kind of fog. 'It was horrible. Like thick clinging soup.'

As soon as the light was switched on all seemed normal again and the street lamp was clearly visible. But the next night the Danks had yet another disturbance. Their bedside lamp began to switch itself off and on again of its own accord.

It was only by chance that the family discovered that their neighbours — whose flat was in the same building — were also having unnerving experiences. One night both couples were having a chat outside when something made them look upwards. They were disturbed to see a face pering down at them from the offices of the Wood Yard next door. (The premises had not been used for months). Although they contacted the owner straight away he arrived to find the door was securely locked. He was amazed to see no trace of footsteps in the grime and sawdust on the floor!

Afterwards Jim — from flat 2 — recalled the night he woke up to find something trying to smother him 'so violently that the bed seemed to be pushed right into the bedroom wall.'

Luckily his muffled shouts alerted his wife, and to his relief the 'thing' vanished without trace.

A few weeks later the Danks family were so thankful to hear they had at last got a house of their own.

But the story doesn't end there. In 1989 the building was demolished and business premises built on the site. (Although some of the former bricks are still to be found in the cellar of the present building). For a time all seemed to be normal, but recently things have 'gone missing' for days — only to reappear on the same spot. No one has touched them. Once again a locked door has opened itself at dead of night setting off the burglar alarm — but the police said they couldn't find a living soul!

The Mystery Bundle

'Whoa there. Steady boy.' Mr. White the grocer held onto his reins and steadied the frightened horse as it shied away from an invisible 'something.' Although there was no breeze and it was a hot summer's day he noticed that the animal was shivering.

What was it all about, he wondered. Was there a pothole in the lane after the recent heavy storm? Was there a rat or a field creature scurrying about beneath them?

Grumbling at the wasted time he climed down from his cart to investigate. There **was** something there. Something wet and soggy. He bent down to look closely. It appeared to be just a dripping wet bundle of rags.

Mr. White was just about to pick it up when his horse whinnied in terror, then before his master could act he bolted away from the scene dragging the cart behind him. For a moment the poor man looked on in horror as its precious contents were spilled all over the country lane. With an effort he was able to catch the trembling animal by the reins and drag it to a standstill.

By the time he had soothed it and left it nibbling peacefully at the grass verge he had decided to return and find out the cause of all the trouble. There was nothing visible on the road, not even a wet patch where the bundle had lain. He could not believe it.

Hours later when he had delivered his goods to Newark market and was taking refreshment at a nearby Hostelry he recounted his adventure.

The landlord was not surprised. 'Oh yes,' he smiled. 'It has been seen before. It's very sad really.' He lowered his voice. 'They say it is the ghost of a boy, a little chimney sweep who drowned in the River Trent.'

The Ghostly Prisoner

Some years ago Arthur, a Newark man, was waiting at the bus stop in Albert Street. He had been standing there in the rain for about twenty minutes waiting for the last town bus. It was cold and uncomfortable and he was beginning to wonder if he had missed it after all.

'Just as I was starting to turn out my pockets to see if I had enough money for a taxi I sensed that there was somebody behind me,' he said. 'I turned to ask if he had seen the bus go past — but my feet seemed to freeze to the pavement.'

'A strange figure was walking towards me dressed in ragged clothes from another age. He was limping badly and I could see one of his thin bare ankles was attached to a length of chain.'

Arthur thought he must be dreaming, or else he was suffering the after effects of his evening at the 'Castle and Falcon.'

'I couldn't believe what I was seeing,' he said. 'I closed my eyes tightly hoping it would go away, but when I opened them again the macabre figure was still there. The most frightening thing of all was that I could see right through him.'

Arthur didn't wait for the last bus, but took off down Albert Street at a run scattering loose change behind him.

'When I was out of breath I stopped for a second beside the old Barracks building and looked behind me,' he frowned, 'but the road was completely deserted.'

N.B. Looking through records of old Newark I discovered that Smith's Brewery in Albert Street is built on the site of the Old Town Gaol.

Who was the ghostly prisoner?

The Ghost of Rose Cottage

You can hardly believe it was once a haunted house, the red bricked cottage, mellow in the evening sunset.

'Rose Cottage' at North Muskham near Newark, used to be occupied by an elderly lady and her daughter. For years they lived there, happy with each other's company, away from the outside world. When the mother died her daughter was inconsolable and became even more of a recluse. Eventually, she could no longer look after herself and moved into a local Nursing Home.

The new owner was enchanted with the cottage, until the trouble started. At first they thought it was the result of bad workmanship when doors opened and closed by themselves. Then door handles were seen to turn even when the family knew the other room was empty. Mysterious footsteps were heard on the stairs when every **human** was downstairs. One night the mother heard footsteps overhead and, thinking it was her children out of bed, went up to settle them. Both children were fast asleep — but she sensed a cold strange atmosphere.

The strangest happening was the weird behaviour of the television set. Night after night it would break down, always at ten minutes to five o'clock. It was thoroughly overhauled but the TV engineer couldn't find a fault.

Weeks later a neighbour remarked that the old lady had always sat with her knitting in the corner where the television now stood. She died there at exactly ten minutes to five!

Months later the family couldn't believe it, ten to five came and went and their TV set was still receiving. They were mystified, until they heard the old lady's daughter had died that night.

Could it be the old lady had been searching for her daughter — and at last they were re-united?

Ghost at the Clinton

Another ghost of a lady in black was seen in Newark only recently and gave the cleaning lady quite a shock.

'For two nights before it happened I couldn't settle at work', said Mrs. Prudence Bombroffe the cleaning lady. 'I had a premonition that something awful was about to happen, and I kept looking over my shoulder as I was working. It was a strange sensation — as though someone was walking behind me. Yet I couldn't hear or see anything unusual.

Prue, a cleaning lady for Barclay's Bank in Newark Market Place, was describing her recent experience.

'The night it happened I went to work as usual in the evening but as soon as I went into the building I could sense an unusual atmosphere.'

'At 7 o'clock she went upstairs to the top floor and started work. Somehow that evening she found it difficult to concentrate. 'Although it wasn't a cold day the temperature up there was freezing,' she said.

While she was busy in the front of the building she heard light footsteps. 'I looked through the open door and saw a grey-haired lady gliding down the corridor. She wore a black dress down to her ankles and a long starched white pinafore. I could see she was carrying a pile of towels in her hand, then she disappeared through the door.'

For a moment Prue was too shocked to move. Then she found the ghost was nowhere in sight. Nobody had seen her going down the stairs.

The building once housed the 'Clinton Arms Hotel' which, in its day, was patronised by Gladstone and Lord Byron. Prue believes her ghost once worked there as a housekeeper or nannie.

'Builders working at the back could have disturbed her,' she said. 'Ghosts don't like change.' She laughed, 'I suddenly realised the date. You won't believe — but it was Halloween!'

The Haunted Battlefield

In June 1987 the village of East Stoke, near Newark, celebrated the 400th Anniversary of the bloody battle of Stoke Fields, where 7,000 men perished in one day. The bitter battle was fought between the armies of Henry VII and supporters of Lambert Simnel pretender to the throne.

Of course the battlefield is reputed to be haunted, but I didn't really believe it — until the day I went to investigate.

It was a winter's day some months before the Anniversary. With two students, Rene and Ann, I set off cheerfully up the lane, cameras in hand, enjoying the rare afternoon sunshine and taking our time. As we turned into the ravine known as the 'RED GUTTER' because it was supposed to have run with blood after the slaughter, there seemed to be an uncanny silence. I could hear the birds singing in the fields around us, but in the RED GUTTER nothing seemed to move.

'What a strange atmosphere,' I whispered to my friends. 'Almost as though it **is** haunted.' I began to look nervously over my shoulder.

'But definitely,' Rene assured me seriously as we started to climb the slope. When I paused to take a photograph he started to relate his experiences. 'Ann and I come here frequently,' he said. 'Many people have spoken of hearing battle cries at night. We have heard noises we can't explain, but the weirdest sounds we've heard are the **whisperings.'**

I began to shiver as my imagination took over. Of course it must be my imagination that was creating the shadowy figure appearing in the lens of my camera.

'Such sad voices,' Ann chimed in, 'sometimes you can hear them all around you. But I was never really frightened of this place until the day I came here by myself.' She went on, 'the car had been playing up so it was almost dusk when I got here.'

I noticed nervously that the sun was going down, casting strange shadows through the trees.

'It was as quiet as it is now, not a breath of wind, then suddenly all the leaves round me started to whirl into the air — like a minature blizzard,' she said. 'After a few minutes it was still again, but the strangest thing was — the tree branches never stirred.' She shivered,' it was so eerie that I turned and ran from the place.'

By now my hands were shaking so much it was difficult to fit my camera back into its case.

'Sometimes if you turn towards the river you get the feeling that someone is pushing you from behind,' Rene told me.

I decided not to experiment. A picture suddenly came into my mind of the thousands of desperate men who had scrambled down the slopes of the RED GUTTER in a vain attempt to reach the river crossing.

'It's too dark for photographs now.' Rene stopped abruptly. 'My friend was taking snaps here last week,' he ventured cheerfully. 'When he looked up he swears there was a naked man watching him. Then he melted away.'

'Probably a Streaker,' I was trying to ignore that shadowy figure I'd seen between the tallest trees. 'Or a Poacher. Yes, That's what it was,' I thought, trying to convince myself.

Ann looked scornful. 'He was carrying a long knife, Jim said. Everyone knows the Irish nobles supporting Lambert Simnel fought naked, apart from their daggers and shields.'

I did not argue. All I wanted was bright lights, civilisation and to enter the 20th century again.

'This way,' the students turned towards the river and I had to follow on. A twig cracked sharply behind me. I moved!

The Mystery Man

The last customer left and the landlord had locked the outside door, to deter 'gatecrashers.' His family and friends had been invited to come in fancy dress, and there was a colourful mixture of pirates, soldiers, fairies, gypsies and many others. The party took place at the 'Lord Nelson' public house in Winthorpe, Nottinghamshire, several years ago.

While the party was in full swing the landlord's son went upstairs to his bedroom. He was surprised, and rather annoyed, to find a 'guest' on his bed. The man was dressed in the uniform of a Cavalier from his be-feathered hat right down to his leather boots.

Thinking what a nerve he had to push his way into a private room he told the man sharply,' I think you had better get back downstairs.'

The man rose from his bed and departed — through the wall! The boy went cold with fright. This was no **ordinary** man.

Through the years things have happened at the 'Lord Nelson' that do not appear to have a logical explanation. Unexplained footsteps have been heard, lights have come on by themselves, and many times the beer taps have turned themselves on and off in the cellar when nobody was down there. The figure of a man has also been seen drifting down the corridor.

When the inn changed hands all was quiet for a while, but recently there have again been antics in the cellar. A former landlady, who was affectionately known as 'Auntie' said it could all be due to the ghost of a soldier. She has actually seen him.

The 'Lord Nelson' was actually built on the site of a former 16th century hostelry called the 'Turk's Head.' I'm told it was mysteriously burnt down. Could the ghostly soldier have been one of its victims?

Chapter V

HAUNTED INNS AND PUBS

The Phantom Piano Player

The 'Spread Eagle' pub in Middlegate, Newark, appeared to have a normal atmosphere — until one unforgettable Sunday morning.

Dennis Hutton who lived there with his parents and grand-parents as a child told me, 'I shall never forget that morning. The whole family were asleep after an extremely busy Saturday night when my Gran was woken up by unexplained sounds. Melodious music was coming from the 'Spread Eagle's clubroom, although she knew the room had been locked up the night before.'

His grandmother quickly roused the menfolk from their beds and the whole family crept along the landing to investigate the clubroom which was also upstairs. They were sure someone had broken in as they could still hear music coming from the piano. The mystery deepened as they found the door was still securely locked.

The moment the door was unlocked the music ended abruptly. The room was in complete darkness until they switched the light on — to reveal an empty room! The piano lid was closed.

'Somehow the very silence made the atmosphere creepy,' Dennis said. 'The room seemed to be icy cold and we couldn't leave it fast enough.'

The phantom piano player didn't give a repeat performance, but weeks later the family heard footsteps in the night and unexplained noises coming from the top of the building.

One night Dennis awoke to hear voices outside his door and saw lights flashing. 'The family had gathered relations together to support them in a "ghost hunt"' he smiled. 'I was told afterwards that no ghosts were seen, but to their amazement the family did find, leading to the roof, a decayed set of stairs they hadn't known about. They were crumbling and dangerous so they were never explored.

Soon afterwards Dennis emigrated to Australia with his family, and still lives there. In 1968 the 'Spread Eagle' was replaced with a fish restaurant. But what happened to the ghostly pianist? Did he also find a new home?

Ghosts at the Lady Bay

When Shirley White, then known as Shirley Fuller, took over the post of landlady of the 'Lady Bay' public house in West Bridgeford, Notts, she little dreamt of the strange events about to take place.

'It was a nice roomy pub,' she said, 'and it seemed just the right size for my son Steve to have his friends in to play while I was busy working.'

Everything seemed to be going well, although Shirley was a little anxious when she started waking in the night to hear strange noises around her. 'At first I thought it was my imagination,' she said. 'Then I began to realise the staff were hearing them too, dis-embodied voices, stairs creaking when nobody was about and whispered conversations that ended abruptly as soon as we investigated the empty landing.'

One night Steve and a friend had been happily playing upstairs on the bedroom floor with his Scalectrix cars, Steve said 'goodnight' to his pal and went back upstairs to switch the set off. After he had just switched the light off he heard a whirring sound. He heard every one of his cars whizzing round the bedroom although he knew the power was off.

'One night our Alsation dogs wouldn't go down the cellar steps,' Shirley said. 'They both stood trembling at the top and refused to move.' After that whenever she closed the doors of the wine cupboards in the cellar at night the staff found them open next morning. It got to a point when her staff dreaded going down there. Some left hurriedly.

The atmosphere became frightening when Shirley was in the Lounge one day and the shadowy form of a monk materialised through the fireplace.

'He had no face,' Shirley shivered. 'He appeared to float across the room and then disappeared.'

Finally a priest was called in to exorcise the pub, and all was well.

Chapter VI

LEGENDS

Does the Angel Weep?

In the village of East Stoke, which lies about four miles from Newark, a very curious legend is related. It is the tale of the angel that is supposed to weep real tears.

East Stoke is built around the cross roads of the Fosse Way, the ancient Roman highway. Most of the village was re-built after the appalling loss of life during the dreaded Plague. Arthur Mee in his book of Nottinghamshire mentions that in the parish register thick black crosses are seen. These mark the deaths of 158 villagers who died there in 1646.

Almost a mile away is the site of the battle of 'Stoke Field' which was fought on June 16th 1487, between the armies of King Henry VII and the supporters of Lambert Simnel, the youth who claimed to be the Earl of Warwick. Here thousands of men were killed all in one day. No wonder the angel is said to weep for them. '

The statue of the angel stands high above the graveyard of the little village church at East Stoke. It is the monument to Baron Pauncefote, who was England's first Ambassador to the United States of America. The Baron died in Washington in the U.S.A. in 1902.

Various stories have been told connected with the statue, including the tale that money can be found on its stone base. (Unfortunately it wasn't my lucky day!)

The face of the angel appears to have a groove running down one of its cheeks, and water was indeed running down it. But who could tell if **real** tears were being shed — for it was raining at the time.

The Witches of Belvoir

'When we were children we used to dare each other to meet up in the grave yard after dark,' Jean, a native of Bottesford near Belvoir, told me. 'There was a story handed down that if we ran round a certain gravestone three times the witch would jump out and grab us. I never plucked up enough courage to do it after the second time.'

The children's story must surely stem from a well known legend in the East Midlands, the gruesome tale of the Flower family who became known as the 'Witches of Belvoir.'

Joan Flowers and her daughters, Margaret and Philippa, worked at Belvoir Castle for the sixth Earl of Rutland and his wife early in the 17th century. The girls were lazy and constantly in trouble with the Countess for their shoddy work. Their mother was little better. She was shunned by her neighbours because of her foul language and evil ways.

Margaret, who worked outside with the hens, became so neglectful that her employer refused to have her working at the castle any longer. Joan Flowers and Philippa grew very abusive and also left their jobs, vowing they would get their own back on the Duke and his family.

The villagers avoided the Flowers even more, whispering behind their backs that the women were dealing with 'familiar spirits' and dabbling in witchcraft.

When the elder son of the Earl, Lord Rosse, suddenly became ill and died in 1613 the parents grieved for him. At that time they had not taken the Flower family's threat of revenge seriously. But when their **second** son also died the earl began to listen to gossip.

The stories of witchcraft flew around the village, especially from the mouths of those who had been threatened by Joan Flowers. Some said that Margaret had stolen a glove from Lord Rosse, stroked the cat (her familiar) with it, and her mother had pricked and buried the glove to bring about the boy's death. Others whispered that the family had associated with other local witches to bewitch and kill his younger brother.

The Earl and Countess waited and listened. Finally they were so convinced by the tales that were being circulated that the Flowers had practised witchcraft. They decided to act. Early in 1619 Joan Flowers, Margaret and Phillipa were under arrest.

Right to the end Joan Flowers protested her innocence. In an arrogant manner she swore that she was not guilty, and that she could prove it. The story is told that on her way to prison she asked for a piece of bread, saying that 'it might never go through me if I am guilty.' The bread choked her straight away and she fell down dead.

With their witch friends Margaret and Phillipa were taken to Lincoln, to be tried by the judges Henry Hobart and Edward Bromley. Apparently the girls confessed to their crime, and were burnt at the stake early in the spring of 1619.

'Just a legend,' you say, or 'I don't believe in witchcraft.' Then take a stroll into Bottesford church, near Belvoir, and you will see the evidence. The grand monument dedicated to the 6th Earl of Rutland, his two wives, and daughters kneeling at their heads and feet. Behind the noble family it is recorded on a large stone scroll how the sons were killed 'by wicked practice and sorcery.'

The Devil Stone

You couldn't mistake it! Childhood memories still remain of the intriguing 'Devil's Stone' which stood outside the village church of Carlton-in-Lindrick near Worksop.

The stone was the subject of weird tales for more than 2,000 years. It was said that it was once an altar dedicated with the blood of human sacrifice, and haunted by 'the ghost of a creature in white.' The ghost of an innocent maiden whose Virgin Blood was sacrificed to appease the gods! After the ghastly deed her mangled body was ceremoniously buried beneath the stone.

Many were the tales handed down of the 'sightings' of the strange spirit near the stone. Some believed it was the devil himself. If the spirit was seen the victim would hastily run round the stone seven times to appease it.

Where the stone came from originally remains a mystery. The stories vary. Some say it was a Monolithic monument, others tell how it was brought from a sacred grove. But all agree — that the devil had a hand in it.

At one time the strangely shaped stone was said to have been **inside** the church — until it was mysteriously removed at dead of night. Shortly afterwards it was again moved out, but no one saw who or what was responsible. Eventually the villagers grew tired of the grim game, and buried it out of sight.

For many years it was covered up, but certainly not forgotten. A local vicar heard the tales and grew curious. With the help of local schoolboys the mysterious stone was unearthed for all to see.

The Haunt of Highwaymen

At one time the ancient 'Blue Bell Inn' at Elston, Nottinghamshire was supposed to be the haunt of Highwaymen. This inn, which dated back to Tudor times, was I'm told a picturesque building with a thatched roof. It stood not far away from the 'Chequers Inn'.

The 'Blue Bell' was given a wide berth when the gentlemen of the road were in the vicinity, for alongside thieves and vagabonds they had found the inn to be the perfect hiding place.

Stories were told in the village of a secret cupboard, similar to a priest's hole, beside the fireplace downstairs which became a refuge after a few crowns had exchanged hands.

Only the landlord knew exactly where to press the panelling in order to reveal the secret opening. What tales he could have told. How anxious to keep on the right side of their host these refugees from justice must have been.

In later years, when the thatched roof was destroyed by fire, workmen repairing the damage and replacing the thatch with modern tiles made an interesting discovery. A gapeing hole in the rafters revealed to them the remains of a concealed trapdoor which led out onto the roof. Could this have been another escape route when the king's men were hot on the trail?

Eventually the 'Blue Bell' became so well known for its notorious 'visitors' that it was closed down, then dis-mantled.

Chapter VII

PREMONITIONS

In 1914 Nellie and Muriel lived with their parents in a small house in Cross Street, Newark. They were a happy and united family — the only sadness in their lives was the absence of their brother Reg, who was away serving with the army in France.

The family wrote to him regularly, but his mud-stained letters from the front were few and far between.

Their mother grew pale and thin as the rumours came to them of heavy fighting in the trenches. The girls watched her sadness hopelessly and tried to help and comfort her.

Then one sunny morning they were pleased to hear her humming a tune as she came home from shopping. She was smiling broadly as she flung open the kitchen door. 'Well, where is he', she said.

They were puzzled. 'Who, mother?'

'Why **Reg** of course,' she started to unload her basket. The sisters

looked at one another in amazement. 'I know he is here on leave. You can't keep it a secret any more.'

Nellie looked bewildered, 'but mother' she began.

'I've seen him outside girls,' she smiled. 'He was coming towards me in his khaki uniform. Don't know why he didn't speak to me, but he touched me on the shoulder and came into the house.'

She started to climb up the stairs calling, 'Reg, Reg, where are you? Come on out wherever you are.'

Although she searched right through the house, to her great sorrow there was no answer.

The telegram came from the War Office the next morning. 'We regret to inform you that your son Reginald was killed in action.'

He had died on the battlefield the previous day.

The Mystery of the Keys

During the last war a girl named Noreen lived with her mother in an old house in Grantham, Lincolnshire. The front section of the house was turned into a grocery shop called 'The Creamery.' In the school holidays Noreen would reluctantly help her mother in the shop, although she wanted to spend every spare moment practising her favourite hobby — dancing.

Monday nights were the pivot of her existance, for on Mondays she was allowed to go dancing with her friend Margaret on the other side of the town.

One night in 1942 Noreen was all dressed up in her 'Glad Rags' as she called them, powdered and smothered in the forbidden make up. (Her mother had already gone out to visit a friend). For some unknown reason Noreen was reluctant to go out even to her beloved dancing classes. However she grabbed her coat when Margaret arrived and they prepared to leave, only to discover a hitch to their plans. The keys of the shop were missing.

"This is ridiculous,' Noreen said after they had made a thorough search of the shop. 'For years mother has always left them in the same place. She never varies.'

Once again the girls looked there, on the high shelf above the door but the keys were still missing. 'We searched every nook and cranny,' she told me, 'until there was nowhere else to look. But there was no sign of them.'

At last the girls reluctantly agreed to stay at home.

'Mother would have killed us if we had gone out and left the door of the shop unlocked,' Noreen smiled.

The next morning we couldn't believe it. 'Where did you say you had looked,' Noreen's mother enquired with raised eyebrows as she lifted the keys from their rightful place on the shelf above the shop doorway!

The girls couldn't believe what they were seeing. 'But that was the first place we looked for them,' Noreen wailed. Her mother took a lot of convincing.

An hour later thay had a visitor. It was a family friend from the far side of town. 'Oh I'm glad to see you are alright,' she sank down onto the nearest chair.

'Why shouldn't we be?'

Their friend stared in disbelief. 'Didn't you hear the plane?' she gasped. 'There was an air-raid down at our side of town'. She shivered 'they are saying several folks were killed late last night.'

Noreen went white as she looked at her mother. 'Oh, mother it was meant to happen,' she sobbed. 'Don't you see. If the keys hadn't gone missing Margaret and I could have been right in the middle of the air raid.'

The Shadow on the Road

When John and his wife Diane were returning to Newark on John's motorbike, after a holiday down south, they little realised the shock that was in store for them.

They had hesitated to take their week in Bournemouth as John's father had been ill for months, but the doctor had assured them that he was 'on the mend.' A relative had offered to move in to keep an eye on him and persuaded them to take a much needed break.

'We were almost halfway home,' John said,' when it started to pour with rain. At the time we were driving down a country road through an avenue of trees. I have to admit I was driving pretty fast. I was so anxious to get home.'

Something told him he must slow down immediately. 'Then a strange thing happened, it seemed unbelievable but we both saw it, the shadowy figure of my father standing on the road in front of us,' John went on, 'It was only for a moment — then he vanished.'

Diane was so shocked that she couldn't speak, but John felt very uneasy. He had a sudden premonition that all was not well. He couldn't get home fast enough.

'When we went in through the gate somehow I could positively sense that there would be bad news waiting for us.'

Sadly John's premonition was right. Anxious relatives had to tell them that his father had died a few hours previously, at the same time he was spotted on that lonely road miles away from his home.

Chapter VIII

CHURCHES, MONKS and ABBEYS

The Phantom Friar

There it was again. Jean Browning wrinkled up her nose as she stood outside the library in the Nottingham General Hospital and the loathsome smell assailed her nostrils. 'It smelled really foul,' she told her friend later. 'The nearest description I could give would be the odour of over-ripe drains.'

When she opened the library door the room was empty except for her friend the Librarian. 'She gave me a wave from her office and turned back to her desk to tidy up,' she said. 'It was then I saw him, the ghost in the library.'

Jean was leaning on the counter waiting for her friend when the room seemed to turn very cold. 'I had the strangest feeling that I was being observed.' She turned quickly and saw the figure of a man in the corner, 'wearing a long habit like the garb of a monk or friar, tied round the middle with a thin girdle. She could see his face clearly. 'His face was flat and broad featured, and his hair appeared to be reddish brown. But the strangest thing,' Jean smiled at the memory. 'He seemed to be walking above the ground as if he had no feet.'

As soon as she spotted him he moved, as though he was attempting to hide behind the book shelves. Jean wasn't at all afraid of him, but had the feeling she had caught him out.

When the Librarian heard Jean call out she went very pale. 'I have known the place was haunted for ages now,' she confessed. 'I've never **seen** him, but so many times I've had the creepy feeling of being watched. 'On other occasions both women smelt that horrible stench again. Although the drains were taken up and the area explored the workmen could find no logical explanation for the smell.

Then the cleaners began to complain that there was something strange in the library although they hadn't been told about the incidents. 'There seemed to be a cold part of the room over there,' one of them complained as she pointed to the opposite corner. 'Whenever I'm working in here I always get the feeling that I must scrub round it.'

Eventually the hospital chaplain agreed to exorcise the ghost. But was that the end of it?

Years later I went to investigate strange happenings at the same Hospital, this time in an empty ward now used by the Spastics Society. Although it was daytime it seemed to have an 'atmosphere' and seemed very unreal without beds, patients and the bustle of the busy nurses.

Stephen George, who works for the society, was operating the photo-copying machine which stands in the one time nurses kitchen. 'I suddenly felt so cold and uneasy,' he said. I turned round sharply in time to see a long rough piece of hessian swirl round just as if someone was standing behind me.'

On another occasion Eileen Sleaford, the Appeals Officer, was working the machine late in the evening. She had bolted the door so nobody could get inside the ward. 'Suddenly I got the feeling that I was not alone,' Eileen said. 'A shadowy figure in a long robe was gliding along the corridor. In a moment it had melted away. I was a bit shaken at the time.'

Records show that a Carmelite Friary did exist nearby at one time. Skeletons and stonework from the Friary have been found between Friar Lane and St. James Street.

Who was the mystery friar? Did he once work on the spot where the hospital now stands, or could it have been his burial ground?

The Haunted Church

A long train journey brought yet another tale of a haunted church. My companian was idly thumbing through her magazine and showed some interest when she came to an article featuring a haunted house. 'Do you believe in ghosts?' she asked me. She was a bit startled at my reaction.

'I had a strange experience during the last war,' she volunteered. 'When I offered to firewatch at my local church in Nottingham, St. George's church in Kirkwhite Street, I wasn't at all worried at the thought of staying alone there all night.'

For a time all went well — then one night she was no longer so confident. It had been quite a night. Even the traffic outside was scarce and the church was quite cosy after the boiler had been stoked up for the night. After the verger had made his last inspection of the building and said 'goodnight' the lady apparently sat reading her book in the dim light until she fell asleep.

.'I woke up suddenly,' she said. 'There had been no noise but for some strange reason I felt uneasy.' She got off her chair and tried the main door into the church. It was still locked, but she had the creepy feeling that she was not alone.

'You are imagining things,' she told herself, and tried to settle down. 'But all the time I could feel a "presence" and then strangely, there was a strong smell of wine.'

Next time her fire-watching stint came round she thought she must have dreamt it all — until the church clock struck midnight. 'I was terrified when I started to hear footsteps going up the aisle, and right up to the altar. I knew nobody else could be in the building.' A foot clicked against the altar rail. Then there was silence. For a moment she was too scared to move, then she ran.

The verger wasn't at all surprised at her tale. 'Oh that's the Reverend X taking Communion,' he grinned. 'he's been haunting us for years.'

The Noisy Ghost

Visitors to Epworth Rectory, the home of John Wesley, include in their tour the bare attic room known as 'Old Jeffrey's Chamber.' Even when visitors are there in daylight it has an atmosphere of its own.

'Old Jeffrey' was the nickname of an old family servant who is supposed to have died there. His ghost is blamed for disturbances to the entire Wesley family. At some time during the early 1700's they all saw him — for he was a noisy ghost.

At first the family must have been alarmed when they heard loud knockings on the doors — and found nobody there. Years later a magazine reported that they had heard noises like the clinking of coins, breaking glass and the heavy clanking of chains.

The family dog was always aware when Old Jeffrey was around — animals are sensitive to ghosts — he must have been un-nerved by the family's response to the strange happenings. How they must have jumped when the door latch moved, the furniture shifted or, worse still, Old Jeffrey appeared.

It seems incredulous that a ghost should haunt such a religious family but even John Wesley was aware of it.

Eventually Old Jeffrey must have tired of pitting his wits against such courage and piety — and — so we believe, quietened down.

The Ghosts of Thurgarton Priory

Thurgarton Priory in Nottinghamshire has been there since the 12th century. Not surprisingly it has gathered its share of legends and ghost stories throughout the years.

Not much remains of the original Priory except the Undercroft — said to be haunted — now part of the building used by 'Boots.' Parts of the old Priory church are also incorporated in the present church.

A man waiting to be interviewed in the Boots building went very white as he called out,' there is a hooded figure of a monk across the room.' His interviewer was not alarmed as the figure had been seen before, but the man was a stranger and was not aware of the tale.

Mr. Logue, another stranger to the district, was driving through the village late one night when a 'figure' appeared in his headlights. He braked sharply, terrified by the bumping of his car and the fear he had run over someone. Then the figure reared in front of him and melted away.

'It gave me a fright,' he shivered. 'I could see it was a monk dressed in a black robe with a large black hood pulled down over his face.'

Several times a 'brown hooded figure' has been seen walking across the fields towards the river at Thurgarton. He is believed to be the ghost of a Layman from the Priory who's duty it was to collect provisions from the boats.

Mr. Roland Huggard owns and lives on a farm once owned by the Priory. He has often heard voices and soft footsteps around him early in the morning. 'They don't bother me,' he smiled. 'I believe it is the ghosts of the monks preparing for their early morning prayers, as they have done for centuries.'

The Ghost of Greestone Stairs

Halfway up Lincoln's Lindum Hill there is a steep flight of stone steps leading to the Cathedral known as the 'Greestone Stairs.' Hundreds of people must have climbed up and down them over the years — I wonder how many of them have encountered the ghostly vicar?

One summer evening a tired nurse was wearily climbing the Greestone Stairs after a long spell of duty on the wards. 'It was twilight,' she said 'and everything seemed to be still. There wasn't even a car on the road below.'

The silence was broken by the voices of her two companions calling 'Wait for us.' She could hear them laughing and chattering to each other as they raced up the steps behind her.

When the nurse turned back to carry on with her climb she was rather startled to find an elderly man standing in front of her. 'He seemed to have materialised from nowhere,' she said. 'It was most uncanny. His eyes seemed to stare at me from a deathly white face.'

Even more startling was his apparel. 'He was dressed in a large black broad-brimmed hat and a black flowing cloak, similar to clothing worn by clergymen in the 17th century.'

When the nurse spoke to him he turned away from her and hurried up the steps. Then she was amazed to see him glide right through the wall in front of her and disappear.

'I thought I must be dreaming,' she said. Then she noticed that her companions had stopped their chattering. 'From the look on their faces I knew they had also seen the ghostly vicar!'

Who Rings the Bell?

It happened in the 'Ringing Room' of St. Giles Church at Balderton near Newark. (This room reached by a short flight of stairs is used by the bell ringers for practice nights — and of course to herald the services). Two years ago Mr. Reed, the Master Ringer, who also has the responsibility for the church clock had a very eerie experience.

As usual, before the ringing of the bells, he arrived early in the evening and locked the door behind him. He climbed up to the ringing room and reached up to adjust the long wire coming from the belfrey above which is attached to the clock mechanism. This wire pulls the clock hammer **away** from the bells when they are about to be rung as they are so heavy.

'On this occasion the wire wouldn't move properly.' he said. 'So I climbed the belfrey steps to the top and released the clock hammer from the rim of the bell by hand.' Then he had such a shock — **someone was pulling the wire from down below!** The wire was being pulled so hard that he had to struggle three times to get the hammer away from the bell. Then, just as suddenly, the pulling stopped.

Although he was shaken Mr. Reed thought quickly and raced down the stairs to intercept the intruder. But the church door was still firmly locked and no one was there!

'During the "happening" there was absolute silence,' he said. 'I hadn't even heard footsteps on the stairs as I would have done if the culprit had been human.' He decided to leave — quickly.

Afterwards he heard the story that a ghostly woman, who has been nicknamed JANE, is supposed to haunt the church belfry.

Another informant mentioned that a midnight reveller saw a 'Grey Lady' passing into the church late one night, but no lights came on inside the building.

Could that have been Jane? Was she the culprit?

Chapter IX

MYSTERIES

The Thing that went Bump in the Night

A bus driver and his conductor were making their way home along the old A57 road in charge of a service bus. All passengers had left at their various destinations. At the time the bus was empty except for the two men concerned, who little dreamt of the shock in store for them.

Both men looked at their watches. 'Five to six, Pete, we're going to be late into Retford unless we get a move on,' the driver remarked increasing his speed as they approached Elksley. The next moment both men gasped. They couldn't believe their eyes.

'Something came out from behind the hedge and floated into the middle of the road,' Pete explained to his workmates later. 'It wasn't a human figure, and it certainly wasn't an animal. More like a dark "shape."'

Before the driver could stop the apparition seemed to appear right in front of the bus. They felt a sickening thump on the bonnet as they hit it full on. Both men heard a terrible scream. Then there was silence.

For several seconds the driver couldn't move, then he scrambled down the steps and out of the bus with trembling legs. Pete followed reluctantly, and they found — nothing and nobody in front of the bus. Certainly no blood stains on the bonnet as they had feared. They walked up and down the road and even looked in the field but the place was completely deserted.

'If we hadn't been together I could have begun to think I had dreamt it all,' the driver said.

Strangest of all when the men finally returned to their bus their watches **still** pointed to five minutes to six!

The incident remained a mystery until months later. Then they were told there was once a fatal accident at that spot. It is believed the 'shape' is the victim — seeking his revenge.

Tale of the Fireplace

When Mrs. Sampson and her husband first moved into Beesthorpe Farm, near Caunton in Nottinghamshire they had the feeling that they were not alone in the house. Surprisingly it did not bother them too much.

Weeks after moving in they were told the place was haunted by the ghost of an old lady who had died in the kitchen. Years before she had become the proud owner of a new black-leaded fireplace, complete with fireside oven and a water container. The old lady was so overjoyed that she told her son, 'I will never ever leave it.'

Mrs. Sampson said that even when the kitchen was eventually converted into a dining-room 'we could feel the old lady's presence. It was a warm friendly feeling and we weren't afraid.'

But their ghostly visitor became restless. They both started to hear her footsteps echoing along the corridor, then one day they heard her climbing the back stairs.

'Night after night we heard her footsteps,' Mrs. Sampson confessed. 'We kept quiet about it until a friend went into the bathroom on her own and hurtled out, shaking with fright, complaining "someone touched me."'

The ghost started tormenting them by turning light switches on and off outside their bedroom door until they couldn't sleep. An electrician investigated in case the switches were faulty. He was puzzled to find no fault.

In desperation the Sampsons called on a priest to exorcise the ghost. The fireplace was dismantled — and all was well.

I cant help having a sneaking sympathy with the old lady who had to break her vow!

The Visitor

Not all ghosts are frightening — as Mrs. Sue Fletcher discovered.

Over twenty years ago Sue's main hobby was piano playing. In time a local choir persuaded her to accompany them at Calverton in Nottinghamshire which she found very enjoyable.

When this choir was invited to give a performance of 'Olivet to Calvary' at their local church the following Easter Sue was delighted for them. Although she was not really familiar with this work she agreed to accompany them at rehearsals. The actual performance was to be accompanied by the resident church organist of St. Michaels.

A week before Easter the organist was suddenly taken ill. Very reluctantly Sue agreed to take his place. She was really worried as she had very limited experience of playing the organ, but didn't want to let the choir down. It was agreed they would practice at St. Michael's Church.

'At that time,' she said, 'there was an old fashioned organ loft, a box-like structure which was situated at the back of the choir seats. After going into the organ loft you had to drop the seats behind you, so there was really only room for the organist.' She smiled, 'the only way I could see what was happening in the church was to glance in the mirror that was hanging above.'

The musical score was more complicated than she had expected. Although she practised daily, to her dismay she couldn't seem to master it on the organ. By Maundy Thursday she was really panicky.

'In desperation I closed my eyes and said a little prayer,' she sighed. 'Then I decided to have one last attempt at it.' It was then that she had a very strange experience.

'Although the heat was on in the church,' she said,' and I was wearing trousers and a warm sweater, I experienced such a feeling of coldness around me that I could have been sitting in a fridge.'

Her hands seemed to go numb although her body was still aware of her surroundings. In a detached way, in her subconscious she knew that something unusual was about to happen.

'At the same time something seemed to tell me that whatever occured I must not look in the mirror.'

Then she heard it, a gentle voice behind her whispering, 'Don't worry. Everything is going to be alright.'

'Even when I felt the pressure of hands on my shoulder I was not afraid,' she said. 'Although I couldn't **see** anybody when I looked round. I knew it would have been impossible for any living being to have squeezed in behind me.'

To her great joy she was able to play the organ perfectly at the performance, and afterwards she was congratulated.

The evening turned out to be a great success. All thanks, she believes, to her unknown 'visitor.'

The Lace-Maker's House

It all began when Iris, the cleaning lady, heard her little grandson call out, 'There's a man outside who wants to talk to you.' Iris, who was working in the old Lace-maker's House at the Park in Nottingham, rushed to the window. She could see the figure of a man standing in the garden below her — but he didn't appear to have any feet!

A familiar voice called up, 'Don't be afraid Iris, I don't wish you any harm.' She recognised the voice of Bill, a former Caretaker.

'It shook me up,' she shivered. 'Bill died only a few weeks before. His voice was so clear he could have been standing beside me, but I knew that nobody else was on the premises.'

Early the next morning the trouble started. She was cleaning the stairs when she heard a door swing to all by itself. Next day she was puzzled when she heard the upstairs toilet flush when she was all alone. When the office staff arrived they could sense an 'atmosphere.' They were all jumpy when a heavy brass door knob suddenly clattered to the floor, eventually they picked it up and left it on the radiator ready for the repairer.

When Iris started work next day the heavy knob came whizzing past her, 'as though it had been thrown by an invisble hand.' Although she was frightened she joker', 'he nearly got me that time.'

A few weeks later Iris jumped on hearing a crashing noise behind her when she was on the ground floor. 'A seven foot fluorescent light tube had mysteriously fallen down and smashed to pieces all over the floor,' she said. 'The weirdest thing was the disappearance of the tall step-ladder when the workmen came to fix the light. The ladder was **always** kept in one place, but they found it had completely disappeared. We searched the whole building. Then I went back to the room we had just searched, it stood in the middle of the floor — I could not believe my eyes. Nobody else had borrowed it.'

Iris was due for more surprises, none of them pleasant. One night when she was cleaning on the top floor she heard the sound of a clock chiming behind her. 'The chimes sounded exactly the same as the clock which stands on the mantlepiece in my home!' Minutes later she was stunned to hear the sound of an object smashing through the office window, followed by more chimes. 'But there wasn't a single clock in the room, and even more scarey — there was no sign of broken glass and the window was still intact!'

Another morning Iris unlocked the door of the upstairs office and found a dead pigeon on the floor. She knew there was no way it could have flown inside as the fireplace had been sealed up for years.

Friends were amazed that Iris seemed so calm, saying, 'Bill doesn't mean me any harm. He's just like a mischevous child.'

Events took a more sinister turn when she arrived in the building at six o'clock one morning when it was still dark. As she switched the lights on and started to climb the stairs, 'someone or something pushed past me and switched them all off.'

Poor Iris was terrified. When the office staff arrived later that morning they were upset to find her still cowering on the stairs in a state of shock.

Iris could not face returning to the Lace-maker's house. Soon afterwards she left Nottingham and went away to nurse a sick relative.

Since she retired all has been peaceful. Of Bill there has been no sign. I wonder if he misses her.

The Burning Bush

A certain vicar, who once lived at nearby Goverton, is still musing over a very strange experience he had one Christmas Eve.

On the night in question the Reverend gentleman had been taking Midnight Mass in St. Peter's Church at Thurgarton in Nottinghamshire. (A church which was built on the site of the ancient Thurgarton Priory). He came out of the building around one o'clock in the morning after everyone had left, and started to drive along the lane from the Priory towards the main road. Suddenly he slowed down. Something strange had caught his eye.

As he looked over to the left, where the ruins of the former chapter House of the Priory are still visible, he could see the vivid glow of a burning bush. 'There was no doubt about it,' he said. 'But I remained in the car. Instinctively I knew that this was no **ordinary** fire.'

He later described it as an 'incandescant glow — like Moses and the burning bush — as distinct from something that had caught fire.'

All night he lay awake pondering over what he had seen. As soon as it was daylight he got into his car anxious to return to the Priory. He was determined to examine the spot where he had seen the vision.

To his amazement he could see no marks of fire where there should have been scorch marks. The ruins were still covered with weeds and grass as though nothing unusual had happened. Yet he **knew** he hadn't imagined it all.

The burning bush has never been seen again but the tale was believed in the village. There is a local belief that it could have been the spirit of another clergyman who once carried out the ceremony of Midnight Mass many years ago.

Martha, the Friendly Ghost

The old farm cottage in their back garden was still being demolished when Mr. and Mrs. Clark moved into their brand new house at Bilsthorpe in Nottinghamshire.

'We were the first owners,' Mrs. Clark said. 'I was so happy arranging our furniture and things to make it into our own home. At first everything was bliss — and then the haunting began.'

At first there were just unexplained noises in the house, the occasional stair creaking in the night, or a door banging. Then came the day when Mr. Clark took his spade and helped to dig up the crumbling foundations of the old cottage. Something made him look up in time to see an elderly lady dressed in a 20th century tweed coat and skirt, a floral headscarf covering her grey hair.

'She stepped out of the ruins of the cottage then glided across to disappear through the walls of our new house,' he shook his head in disbelief, 'It was quite uncanny.'

The young couple saw their elderly guest many times. It was as if they had disturbed her from her new home. They nick-named her 'Martha'. Then the noises began.

'I have never heard anything quite like it,' Mr. Clark said. 'It was a peculiar vibrating noise that seemed to shake the whole building. It always seemed to be loudest on the landing, and we noticed that it always occured on the night of the full moon.'

Mr. Clark, a level headed college lecturer, tried to reason that there must be a practical explanation for the noise. One particularly noisy night he turned the electricity off and tried to record the noise with a meter, but although the vibration was still there the meter **could not record it!** It remains a mystery.

Soon afterwards the couple grew tired of the constant disturbances and moved to a house several miles away. The first few days were so peaceful it seemed as if they would have no more trouble. Then it began again — not the vibrating noise — but strange creaking on the stairs, and the sound of shuffling footsteps.

'We didn't actually see Martha again,'Mrs. Clark smiled. 'But we got the impression that she had followed us.'

Doors opened by themselves, and on two occasions she was amazed to see the cushion depressed on the chair in front of her, as though some visible person had just sat on it.

A visitor to the house alleged that a towel swung off the towel rail towards her when she was getting out of the bath, which gave her a bit of a shock. (Martha was definitely trying to be helpful).

'In time we stopped worrying about her and took it in our stride,' Mrs. Clark explained. 'So much so that one day I got really annoyed when she was up to her tricks, and shouted "For goodness sake close the door behind you."'

Much to her astonishment the door handle came down — and the friendly ghost obeyed.

N.B. The experts have suggested that the mysterious vibrating noises were caused by ancient LEY LINES that could be running under the house.

But that is another story.

Polly Blackman's Pond

Years ago there was a pool of water situated just outside Winthorpe, in Nottinghamshire, that was known locally as 'Polly Blackman's Pond.'

A tale is told in the village that during the eighteenth century a local woman named Polly Blackman and her husband were returning to their house in nearby Holme village when they 'vanished.'

The story goes that Polly and her spouse had been seen travelling along Holme Lane in a carrier's cart after a profitable day at Newark Market. Maybe they were tired, or maybe they had celebrated a little too well and let the old horse have his own way, to accidentally stray from the road into the murky waters. They were never seen again.

How could a full size cart disappear into a village pond without trace? How could a horse stumble over the edge without leaving imprints of its hooves on the ground? Why did nobody hear a scream, or a splashing from the water? The mystery remains unsolved.

On a bright summer's day I searched for Polly Blackman's Pond — which is supposedly near Winthorpe's cricket ground. The pond had long since been carefully filled in. Does that place still guard a sinister secret?

The Haunted House

The table started to move all by itself. Lisa was terrified . . . .

It all started when Lisa and her sister Charlotte went to live in a Manor House near Aslockton, Notts., with their parents.

At first the family were delighted with the rambling old house, which had once been divided into three cottages. All went well until the mother woke up feeling she was being watched. Suddenly she began to have difficulty with her breathing, as she gasped a woman materialised in front of her in a grey misty gown of a bygone age. Before the girl's mother had recovered from the shock the figure vanished. Several nights later the spectre appeared to her again.

At first the family were sceptical, until Lisa also had a frightening experience. She was alone in the dining-room, in the middle of the house, when the huge oak dining table started to move. Lisa was amazed to see it lift itself from the floor and float around the room. When she tried to make a dash for the door the table jammed against it. She was terrified. For moments she couldn't get out. The room was icy cold and full of fear.

Lisa thankfully heard her mother coming after she had screamed. As soon as the door handle moved the table tipped back onto its side. (Where the removal men had left it earlier).

While the mother was away one night, the girl's father awoke in the night shivering. He saw the same ghostly woman standing by his bed, pulling at his bedclothes. As the family, hearing his shouts, came to his aid the ghost vanished. He found it a truly horrifying experience.

Visitors to the house became frightened when they felt an invisible 'someone' touching their hair, and they left hurriedly.

In desperation the family consulted the Ouidji Board. 'Is this house haunted?' they asked. The glass spelt out Y E S . They were all startled when the name BELL appeared. The name meant nothing to them.

Weeks later they mentioned the name to the church warden. After a pause he told them,' a family of that name once lived in a cottage that was the middle part of your home. It was very tragic, as one day the cottage caught fire and neighbours were only able to rescue three of the family. The fourth member was never found.'

Charlotte and Lisa realised that their haunted bedroom and dining room had been part of the fated cottage. Things were beginning to fall into place.

Then odd things started to happen to their pet dog, affectionately known as 'Sixpence.' She started to go hysterical for no apparent reason, although she had formerly been a placid animal. It was the final straw when Sixpence went missing. After a long search they were upset to find her jammed into a bucket in the well in their garden..

Charlotte said, 'We knew she wouldn't go near it on her own. She was terrified of water,'

The whole family decided to move away from the village.

Months later the sisters decided to re-visit their old home. They found the new owners were also having trouble. Once again the family dog had been the victim of the 'hauntings.' He was found dead under mysterious circumstances. Their small child kept asking, 'who is that lady?' when the room appeared to b empty.

Out of curiousity the sisters explored the graveyard. They found **three** graves belonging to the Bell family — of the fourth there was no sign!

Chapter X

THEATRE GHOSTS

Ghostly happenings in the theatre are numerous. Many theatres have long histories and, not surprisingly, are haunted by actors who once performed in them.

However, a ghost with a difference has been sighted at the 'Bonington Theatre' in Nottinghamshire.

A Ghost Takes the Stage

A skull and several bones that were found prior to the opening of Arnold's Leisure Centre may have a connection with the nocturnal visit of a local ghost. The grisley find was discovered when excavations were carried out before the foundations of the centre commenced.

Who the ghost is and where he came from remains a mystery, but for some time people have reported 'goings on' at the centre's neighbouring Bonington Theatre.

During the daytime the ghostly visitor keeps a low profile I am told, but at nightime after the performance is over and the audience have gone home, unexplained footsteps have been heard coming from inside the theatre although it is securely locked.

The discovery of the sinister skull and human bones, with a little research, revealed that at one time a Quaker community had worshipped in that area. The theatre could possibly have been built on their burial ground. Could the footsteps belong to the ghost of a reckless Quaker?

Uninvited Guests at the Robin Hood

The 'Robin Hood' Theatre at Averham, near Newark was created from the shell of an old barn. Although it stands in the countryside, audiences come from miles to support its excellent productions. They say the old theatre has a 'warm friendly atmosphere.' But that was not always so.

Years ago a young group of players calling themselves the 'Bristol Theatre Players' came to the Robin Hood. Being dedicated and eager they arrived the night before and started to rehearse. It was then that they started to have problems.

'Props began to go missing,' actor Ian Rogerson told me. Furniture was moved around without anyone touching it and some people were getting heated and blaming each other for things that were going wrong.'

The weirdest happening was the unexplained behaviour of a large light fitting in the ceiling. 'Sensing that there was a shadow up above me,' Ian said, 'I looked up and was amazed to see the whole light fitting turning around.'

The electrician went up to test it, but found that the fitting was fixed quite firmly in place.

Fortunately everything went as planned on the night of the Bristol Theatre Company's production, and it was definitely a case of 'alright on the night.' Apart from a small incident.

As the company were leaving the theatre after celebratory drinks, the producer insisted that the doors were carefully locked and all the lights switched off. The theatre's cleaning lady was the last to leave. As the company started to pile into their cars they heard a shout. They all rushed back to find — every light in the theatre had switched itself on.

Return of the Actor

'He shot out of the cellar as though old Nick himself was after him,' Joe laughed. 'The poor chap was obviously scared. He was as white as paper.'

'Perhaps he'd seen a ghost?' I said hopefully getting my pen and notebook at the ready.

Joe stared at me thoughtfully. 'Now how did you know that?'

Then the story came out. Apparently Joe Clark and his mate were getting ready for knocking off time at their job in the Electricity Showrooms when their distressed workmate appeared. Even after a lot of 'leg pulling' from friends he insisted that he had seen a ghost.

'I **did** see him,' he said. 'It was the ghost of a little boy, wearing a green velvet suit with white collar and cuffs — and he had black curly hair.' He shuddered, 'I couldn't see his face properly, but as soon as I shouted he faded away into nothing.'

Although that happened many years ago other people have seen him — but not recently. They believe he was the ghost of a child actor.

In 1774 a theatre was erected on the spot where the Electricity Showrooms, in Middlegate, Newark, now stand. The theatre increased in popularity and even produced acts from the 'Drury Lane' in London.

But in later years the theatre had its ups and downs. The Robertson family, who ran it for many years, got into debt and Mr. Robertson was in prison for a time. Audiences, as in modern times, fluctuated and the theatre was closed and re-opened more than once.

A Hurricane caused heavy damage in 1839, but still the theatre struggled on. It was finally demolished in 1884.

I wonder, what part did the little ghost boy play in the history?

Footsteps in the Night

The older theatres, by their reputations, appear to be the perfect hunting grounds for resident ghosts. The Theatre Royal at Nottingham is one of them.

A clairvoyant who visited the theatre one night was convinced that the theatre **was** haunted. He believed that the ghost of a cleaning lady was still around and needing help. The message came over to him that the girl had worked at the theatre early in this century, and had lived nearby — until she died tragically and suddenly.

Ann Buckley, who worked at the theatre for a time also believed that the theatre had its ghosts. She noticed staff were not all that keen on being left on their own in the theatre at night.

'After the audience have left, the voices stilled and the bright lights dimmed, the theatre takes on a very different atmosphere,' she said.

One of her workmates had a fright one night just as she was about to leave. From the Dress Circle — which was all in darkness — she could hear the echo of footsteps walking round and round. Yet she knew the theatre was completely empty. She rushed out leaving her coat behind.

A member of the stage crew had a lucky escape one evening when heavy fire axe whizzed passed the spot where he had just been sta⌐
Luckily he wasn't hurt, but very shaken, 'I couldn't underst⌐

shivered, 'We always kept it up in the flies. We knew it was securely fastened.'

Final proof can be seen in the book 'Theatre Royal Nottingham, 1865 to 1978' which contains a 19th century photograph of a horse and carriage taken outside the Theatre Royal by an astonished theatre-goer. What a shock he must have had, to see the ghostly horse without a head!

The Man in Grey

A mystery surrounds the exquisite little theatre at Chesterfield, in Derbyshire, known as the 'Pomegranate Theatre.' The theatre was built in 1898, and was an extension of the Memorial Hall erected in memory of that great rail engineer, George Stephenson.

The ghost of a 'grey man' dressed in what seems to resemble a dark frock coat, has been seen several times by startled cleaners. He usually appears on the balcony walking left to right. Frequently he sits down on one of the red plush seats.

From the start the ghost has been known as 'George.' Some say it is the ghost of George Stephenson himself. (He ended his days at his home, 'Tapton House' which stands only a short distance from the theatre).

A former Stage Manager often heard footsteps going across the stage when he was alone in the theatre. Each time he complained 'the theatre seemed to go suddenly cold.'

A curtain has moved by itself when the Chief Technician has been working late at night on his own. 'If the ghost is around I know things will go wrong,' he laughed. 'One night I was just going out of the stage door after turning the lights off when I felt a drop in temperature. As soon as I had locked up outside I saw them all come on again. 'George' was at his tricks.'

Actor/Director Leslie Orton believes in the ghost. One afternoon he was sitting on the balcony adjudicating a Drama Festival. 'Suddenly I knew George was standing behind me. When I turned he had vanished.' On another occasion, Leslie was alone in the theatre preparing for the show, 'Fiddler on the Roof.' 'Although I was wearing headphones I could tell the ghost was there,' by the freezing atmosphere.' he laughed. I looked up and said, 'Go away George.' My script moved as though someone was passing by — then the air was warm again.'

Chapter XI

ANIMAL GHOSTS

Ghostly Cats

In the animal world cats, for all their nine lives, have a habit of turning up as spirits; Maybe because of the many tales of cats being connected with the practice of witchcraft.

In his book of 'Legends and Folklore' John Merrill tells the story of a field in Leigh, Worcs. where the hounds chased **'something** no-one could see' eventually discovering the 'something' to be a local witch who had taken the form of a cat.

One such tale appeared in my last book 'Ghosts and legends of Newark,' about the old witch of Sutton on Trent, near Newark, who haunted a local family disguised as a 'great ugly cat.'

Ethel Rudkin, in 'Lincolnshire Folklore' reveals the story of a ghostly cat of abnormal size that haunted Commonpiece Lane near Gainsborough said to be 'white and nearly as large as a pig.'

I'm told that the people of Radford in Nottinghamshire caused a stir when they reported that they had been frightened by an invisible cat that rubbed against their legs without warning. At first nobody would believe them, putting the phenomena down to their imagination. Until the day the local 'Bobby' was sent to investigate, and to his astonishment actually felt the ghostly animal weaving around him.

During the 1970's Mrs. Cooke-Chambers was amazed to see a black cat making its way down her staircase at Winthorpe, near Newark. When it got to the bottom step it vanished. Members of the 'Sealed Knot Society' visited the Hall and they also saw 'the ghost of a cat' strolling in the grounds.

The Ghost of Cymba

For many years Carol and her husband, who lived in an isolated house near Southwell, Notts, kept an Alsation called Cymba. The dog was loved and treated like a member of the family, never leaving their side.

Carol was heartbroken when Cymba died, and in spite of her husband's offer to buy a new puppy to console her vowed that she would never have another dog in the house. 'No other dog could take her place,' she said. But as her husband worked away from home that winter she was eventually persuaded to buy a new dog for 'protection' while she was alone.

Soon after Amber, an endearing golden-haired Retriever, came to the house Carol had an uneasy feeling that all was not well. 'I couldn't put my finger on it,' she said, 'but there seemed to be a peculiar atmosphere in the house. I sometimes had the feeling that I was being watched. Then one night when I settled down by the fire I was astonished to see Cymba sitting in the hallway.'

In a moment the dog had vanished, but a few weeks later Cymba again appeared to her beloved mistress. 'I was never able to touch her, but somehow it comforted me to know that her ghost was still there,' Carol said. 'We wondered why she always appeared when Amber was around — then I noticed that Amber's dog-lead, food-bowl, and an old pair of slippers that she played with kept being moved about. It suddenly struck me that Cymba was jealous.'

Gradually normality returned to the house and there was no sign of the 'doggie ghost.'

But occasionally Amber, the Retriever, grows restless and wags her tail frantically for no apparent reason. Is she still being watched?

Mystery of the Black Dog

The stories of ghostly black dogs seem to be fairly common. A few months ago I had a strange experience which led me to believe one such ghost could be haunting right here in Nottinghamshire.

It happened on a bright sunny day in August. Friend Barbara and I were returning in her car from Derbyshire when we both saw a large black dog about to cross the road in front of us. Barbara had plenty of time to avoid it, and we thought no more about it.

However we were startled some time later when a black dog again dashed in front of us **from the same side.** The car was by then travelling fast, and there was no way a dog could have travelled at the same speed and at that distance. We both felt uneasy and cold even in the bright sunshine.

Both times we had seen the dog approaching. 'It can't be the same one.' I spoke aloud to reassure myself. After that we were both on the alert and scanning both sides of the road when the black dog appeared — apparently from nowhere — **right in front of the car!** Barbara had to slam the brakes on so fast that all our luggage tipped off the back seat onto the floor.

It was broad daylight but I have never been so frightened in my life. Although we immediately jumped out of the car there was no sign of the dog.

Afterwards I realised, we were outside the grounds of Newstead Abbey which is haunted by the ghost of Byron's pet dog, Bosun.

Chapter XII

EVEN MORE GHOSTS

The Phantom Stage Coach

Many strange tales have been related of the ancient fens of Lincolnshire. One such was told of an incident that occured to Mr. Bob Smith, more than 40 years ago.

Bob was driving home slowly through Lincolnshire late one night after a meeting with old friends. He was 'not drunk, just pleasantly merry.' He was driving along a road near Digby Fen, a road which he said 'is absolutely straight so it is possible to see oncoming traffic from a good distance.' It was dark, though a starlit night, and he was just thinking how isolated the district was when he saw two bright lights twinkling towards him along the road.

'In those days there were far more cyclists than Motorists on that road,' Bob Said. 'I slowed down slightly to let the 'cyclists' as I though they were, more room to pass my car. I was surprised when the lights suddenly disappeared.'

He drove on cautiously thinking the vehicles must have turned down a side road, but further on it became obvious that there was no side turning to be seen, and no sign of a car or bicycle.

'Something gave me goose-pimples,' he shivered. 'I worried about it all the way home. It was uncanny the way those lights disappeared'.

Next day he phoned a friend who lived in the fen district. The friend laughed loudly when Bob told his tale.

'That was no bicycle,' he said. 'That place is haunted. You saw the lights of the phantom stage-coach.' He lowered his voice. 'They say that in the 18th century a stage-coach was lost in the fog and disappeared without trace.' He paused dramatically. 'Years later they found it deep in the Bog.'

The Tale of the Plough Blade

For this tale I am indebted to Mrs. Harding from Wollaton Hall Industrial Museum.

During the summer of 1980 a family in Bramcote Moor, Nottinghamshire, were busy creating a new garden when the spade hit upon something hard. They were quite disappointed when they found it was only an old Plough Blade. So it was casually thrown aside until evening. When it began to get dark they went inside leaving the blade propped up between the two houses, and forgot all about it.

During the night the families in both houses experienced 'happenings' simultaneously, but unknown to each other. In both houses voices were heard in the night. Footsteps were heard upstairs when nobody was visible. The unexplained noises were so frightening in one house that a mother ran outside leaving her innocent children asleep in bed.

Eventually professional outside help was called in from Nottingham University to investigate. It was later discovered that a farmer's wife who had lived in the area years ago had been involved in a horrific accident on the farm, and had been badly maimed by a plough. Tragically the poor woman was driven to take her own life.

People living on the site have seen her from time to time. The doors of their homes have occasionally opened late at night without warning.

However people gradually stopped being afraid when they realised the ghost brought no bad feelings with her.

Eventually the families in the adjoining houses were advised to bury the old plough blade where they had found it. After doing so they were left in peace.

The Dog that Laughed

The Manor was a very large rambling old house situated in a village outside Nottingham. Rumour had it that it was haunted by the ghost of a lady who had died there in the 18th century.

Jock didn't take much notice when he first went to work there. he didn't really believe there were such things as ghosts. If there were it wouldn't bother him. He was more bothered about the tales of vandals in the district and about his responsibility. He was employed as caretaker to the Manor while alterations were taking place. It was being turned into a school.

In the daytime he was surrounded by workmen banging and hammering, enough to frighten any ghosts away. At night he was cozy in his flat over the stables — and he had his faithful terrier Floss beside him. It was a good life, he only hoped they would keep him on when the school took over.

Every evening at dusk Jock and Floss walked round the grounds to make sure all was well. One night they were about to turn in when Floss stopped suddenly and started to growl. There was something moving in the bushes.

'Go get them Floss,' Jock urged, wondering if somebody was after the building materials. Tu his amazement Floss started to tremble and backed away. He could see a woman's face peeping out.

'Hi,' Jock shouted. 'You're trespassing.' The face vanished. Although he searched the bushes thoroughly nobody was there. 'That's odd.' Jock turned to see his faithful dog streaking across the lawn as though the devil himself was after her.

After a hearty supper and a good nights sleep Jock forgot all about the incident.

A week later he started out on his rounds as usual. 'Come on lass' he urged as Floss cowered in the corner. For some reason she seemed very reluctant to go outside. Muttering under his breath Jock strode out leaving the door open. Floss slunk out keeping well behind him. 'Beautiful night.' Jock observed the moonlit garden. He was just having a final puff on his pipe when he saw the silhouette of a grey lady outlined against the summer house. By the time Jock had turned round the woman had gone. Floss uttered a yelp of terror and shot into the house.

'Must have been a trick of the light,' he tried to reassure himself when he was telling the builders next day.

'You want to watch it Jock,' the foreman laughed. 'It's old Meg, she's after you.'

'Ghosts man,' Jock grinned. 'Don't believe in all that rubbish.'

And he didn't, not really, until a few nights later when he saw the woman again. He was standing by the stables when he became aware of a smell of lavender, so strong it overpowered his tobacco smoke. 'Must be coming from the garden after the rain,' he told Floss. She was standing absolutely still. 'What is it lass?'

He was startled when he saw the grey figure of an old lady coming towards them. She was limping badly and leaning on a stick. As she came closer pity overcame his fear when he saw her thin twisted body. She bent over to pat Floss then —

'You wouldn't believe it lads,' he told his captive audience next day. 'The old dog's tail started wagging, she rolled over on her back and — the look on her face.' He shook his head in disbelief. As true as I'm standing here, I'll swear that my Floss was laughing.'

Night Nurse

In the past, Nottingham General Hospital has been the scene of many hauntings, according to student nurse Bob Anthony. 'The strangest 'happening' was the ghostly Night Sister's round,' he said. 'Even now it is difficult to believe.'

Apparently he experienced this in the MABEL PLAYER ward, the round shaped ward, now empty, at the top of the hospital building.

'If we had a quiet night when patients were asleep we were able to relax a little,' he smiled. 'Of course we always kept an ear open in case of an unexpected visit from Sister.'

The first time they heard unfamiliar footsteps coming up the well of the stairs they 'got busy,' thinking it was the lady in question. 'We heard the footsteps reaching the top step and through a panel in the glass door I could see letters on the notice board outside rustling as though someone was walking past — but I couldn't **see** anyone. The door opened quietly, by itself, but nobody came in.'

The staff looked at one another in horror, they could hear soft footsteps going round the ward but none was visible. Yet they could plainly see the charts wafting about at the end of the patients beds as though someone had just passed by them. Each time the footsteps stopped they noticed the charts were still. 'Just as if an invisible member of staff was checking each patient's chart in turn.'

When the footsteps had gone all round the round-shaped ward the staff witnessed the door opening by itself again, notices fluttering, and heard the sharper sound of footsteps 'tap, tapping' as they echoed down the stone stairs. 'It was really weird,' Bob shivered as he remembered.

'Another strange incident took place in the former HOGARTH WARD,' Bob told me. 'I remember vividly a night when there were only two of us on duty. We were rushed off our feet that night trying to cope with an influx of patients. I could see that a seriously ill patient wanted his drip renewing, but I remember thinking I would have time to do another job in the five minutes before I needed to change the bottle.'

When Bob dashed back to the patient he couldn't believe his eyes. The empty bottle had been replaced with a full one. 'I thanked Jill the other nurse for helping me out and she knew nothing about it. No other member of staff had been in the ward.'

The ghostly 'helper' seemed to have had a busy night for later in the evening there was another odd occurence. 'Things were still a bit hectic,'

Bob laughed. 'It seemed like the last straw when a patient shouted out that he must have a bottle to wee in **at once.** I could see he was desperate but at that moment I wasn't able to leave another very sick man. 'In a minute' I shouted.'

When at last Bob dashed back with a bottle the patient was smiling. 'It's OK mate,' he beamed. 'The nurse in the funny clothes saw to me.'

'Which nurse?' Bob was puzzled.

'Never seen her before. She was dressed in a grey uniform covered by a long white pinafore that went down to the ground, and she was wearing a sort of frilly hat.'

The uniform he described was worn by nurses in the hospital when it FIRST opened in the 1780's.

A Night of Terror

It was a nightmare. Every time she tried to reach the door it was there, rubbing against her . . . .

When Eileen the cleaner started work at the bank in Bulwell, Notts., everything seemed straight forward. She assured her employers that it would not worry her to be working alone in the building at night. She was not afraid of the dark, and she was so grateful to have the chance of a part-time job while her children were so small. For weeks Eileen followed her routine and was glad to have the building to herself, after caring for two lively youngsters in the daytime. But that all changed one unforgettable evening.

That night Eileen locked the outer door as usual and started to sweep down the corridor. For some unknown reason she was reluctant to open the door to the staff common room. When she finally went inside she couldn't believe what she was seeing. A strange white glow was coming from the top of the coffee table, although the rest of the room was in darkness. Eileen managed to switch the light on — then the room seemed quite normal. She decided to phone her friend for comfort. As she picked up the phone she heard a 'click' and the kettle switched itself on.

'I rushed over to switch it off,' she frowned. 'The moment my back was turned it started boiling again.' Even when she pulled the plug from the wall it started up again. 'Then I heard a terrible crashing noise, and then silence.'

The silence unnerved her most of all after what had happened. 'The atmosphere terrified me. I couldn't wait to get out.'

But there was worse to come. As soon as she tried to get out of the room she was horrified to feel something rubbing against her. 'Every time I moved it was there, like a big cat weaving in and out of my legs — but the room was empty.' Finally she managed to race down the corridor and out into the night, afraid to look behind her.

ACKNOWLEDGEMENTS

I would like to give my grateful thanks to the following

Dennis Hutton

Tom Ellerton

'Lincolnshire Life Magazine'

Barbara Ward

Barbara Watt

Roland Hoggard

Shirley White

Margaret Whittaker

Ann Buckley

Mrs. Creed

Ruth Mackintosh

Joan Wallace

Ann Bombroffe

Ron and Frank

Joan Fretwell and Elsie Rayner

Norah Lunn

Kath Danks

Miss White

Mrs. Peatfield

Noreen Millar

Mr. Reed

Mrs. Sampson

Charlotte Gradon

Mrs. Buxton

Mrs. Sue Fletcher

Jean Cox

Eileen Sleaford

Bob Anthony

Staff of Harvest Bakery

Les Smith